Foreign Aid
to
End Hunger

Hunger 2001

Eleventh Annual Report on the State of World Hunger

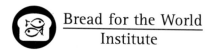

Bread for the World
Institute

50 F Street, NW, Suite 500
Washington, DC 20001
USA

printed on recycled paper with soy inks

Bread for the World Institute

President
David Beckmann

President Emeritus
Arthur Simon

Director
Richard A. Hoehn

Editor
Joanna Berkman

Co-Editor
Asma Lateef

Project Assistant
Lori Metcalf

Design
Dennis & Sackett Design, Inc.

©2001 by Bread for the World Institute
50 F Street NW, Suite 500
Washington, DC 20001
Telephone: (202) 639-9400   Fax: (202) 639-9401
E-mail: institute@bread.org
Website: www.bread.org

Printer: HBP, Hagerstown, MD

Cover photos counter-clockwise from top left: Margie Nea, FAO, FAO, Jim Stipe

Manufactured in the United States of America
First Edition Published in February 2001
ISBN 1-884361-09-9

Table of Contents

Acknowledgments

We are deeply grateful for the valuable insights provided by our sponsors, co-sponsors, and colleagues who attended our April 2000 consultation and who reviewed various drafts of the manuscript:

David Atwood – USAID; Steve Arnold – American University; Lynn Brown – World Bank; Edward Chesky – consultant; Marc Cohen – IFPRI; Don Crane – ACDI/VOCA; David Devlin-Foltz – Aspen Institute; Eugenio Diaz-Bonilla – IFPRI; Jennifer Douglas – USAID; Ginger Doyel – University of Richmond; Buzz Guroff – ACDI/VOCA; Edward Heinemann – IFAD/Rome; Douglas A. Hicks – University of Richmond; Lynne Jurgielewicz – Catholic Relief Services; Perry Letson – ACDI/VOCA; Anthony Matthews – IFAD/Washington, DC; Marty McLaughlin – Center of Concern; Walter Owensby – PC(USA); Rajul Pandya-Lorch – IFPRI; Rachelle Schlabach – Mennonite Central Committee; Sue Schram – USAID; Art Simon – President Emeritus, Bread for the World; Meena Venkataramu – University of Richmond; Vera Weill-Halle – IFAD/Washington, DC; Margaret Zeigler – Congressional Hunger Center.

We very much appreciate those who critiqued and contributed to various drafts of Chapter 6:

Jennifer Davis – former director of the Africa Fund; Doug Tilton – South African Council of Churches; Jim Cason – La Jornada; Imani Countess – Africa Policy Information Center.

We thank the researchers, writers, and consultants upon whose work and assistance this volume relies:

Bias Arrudão – consultant; David Atwood – USAID; Sika Awoonor – GoodWorks International; Jelle Bruinsma – FAO/Rome; Cathy Cooper – consultant; Raymond Copson – Congressional Research Service; Donald Buckingham – University of Ottawa; David Devlin-Foltz – Aspen Institute; Filippo Dibari – IFAD/Rome; Father Ricardo Figueira Rezende – Human rights activist/Brazil; Richard Forrest – U.S.-Japan Common Agenda Public-Private Partnership (InterAction); Juanita Frazier-Martin – The Rockefeller Foundation; Mary K. Garber – consultant; Lisa Greenwood – USDA; Lori Heninger – Quaker United Nations Office; Douglas A. Hicks – University of Richmond; Howard Hjort – consultant; Davidson Jonah – Christian Children's Fund; Samuel Kasankha – African Writers' Project/Zambia; Coretta Scott King – Martin Luther King Jr. Center for Nonviolent Social Change; Steven Kull – PIPA; Charles MacCormack – Save the Children; Anthony Matthews – IFAD/Washington, DC; Eugene McCarthy – consultant; Evelyn Mills – U.S. Department of Health and Human Services; Larry Nowels – Congressional Research Service; Toni L. Radler – Christian Children's Fund; John Ruthrauff – Oxfam America; Don Reeves – consultant; Duncan Samikwa – European Food Security Network/Malawi; Joseph Kalungu Sampa – Structural Adjustment Policy Monitoring Project/Zambia; Joyce Sampson – Academy for Educational Development; Chris Schoessler – IFAD/Washington, DC; John Schultz – Christian Children's Fund; Isaac Shapiro – Center on Budget and Policy Priorities; Steven Sinding – Columbia University; John M. Staatz – University of Michigan; Eileen Stillwaggon – Gettysburg College; John Teton – International Food Security Treaty Campaign; Jeronimo Tovela – National Union of Peasant Farmers/Mozambique; Flavio Valente – ÁGORA/Brazil; David Weiner – Overseas Development Council; John Westley – IFAD/Rome; Laura White – World Relief; Margaret Zeigler – Congressional Hunger Center.

The following Bread for the World members and BFW and BFW Institute staff provided articles, comments, and assistance:

Ray Almeida, Kathleen Bulger – Mickey Leland Hunger Fellow, Kimberly Burge, Bill Connelly, Jermaine Cruz, Janet Hodur, Larry Hollar, Barbara Howell, Diane Hunt, Michael Kuchinsky, Karin Lyttkens-Blake, Henry Maingi, Elena McCollim, Jim McDonald, Tom Murphy, Kathy Pomroy, Howard Salter, Stephanie Seidel, Jim Stipe, Will Stott, Bob Tiller, Ben Turner – Mickey Leland Hunger Fellow, Joel Underwood, Rebecca Vander Meulen, Tammy Walhof.

Themes of Annual Reports on the State of World Hunger

Bread for the World Institute

Hunger 2000: A Program to End Hunger

Hunger 1999: The Changing Politics of Hunger

Hunger 1998: Hunger in a Global Economy

Hunger 1997: What Governments Can Do

Hunger 1996: Countries in Crisis

Hunger 1995: Causes of Hunger

Hunger 1994: Transforming the Politics of Hunger

Hunger 1993: Uprooted People

Hunger 1992: Ideas that Work

Hunger 1990: A Report on the State of World Hunger

Summary

The United States could lead an international movement to reduce world hunger by half by 2015, a goal set at the 1996 World Food Summit. In partnership with developing countries, the United States and other industrial nations have the resources to make it happen.

U.S. aid has had many notable successes that can serve as models for working with developing countries. The Marshall Plan helped Europe and Japan rebuild after World War II. The Green Revolution doubled crop yields and cut hunger by more than half in Asia. The UNICEF Child Survival Initiative, partially funded by U.S. foreign aid, saves the lives of 4 million children a year through low-cost immunizations and oral rehydration therapy.

Foreign aid clearly works when it is well planned and funded. At least 25 countries that once received development aid have become self-sustaining. Some, like Japan, are wealthy enough to give aid to other nations.

Unfortunately, U.S. foreign aid has not always helped hungry people. Much U.S. aid in the Cold War era was for military or geopolitical purposes, propping up anti-communist governments (even dictatorial, corrupt, or incompetent ones) in the developing world. Relatively little U.S. aid has been targeted to development that could end hunger and poverty in the world's poorest countries.

Because of these past mistakes, some people in the United States are skeptical about the effectiveness of foreign aid. Nevertheless, a new poll released in this report indicates that 87 percent would favor a targeted program to reduce hunger in the developing world.

The poll also shows that most people think the U.S. gives 20 times more in foreign aid than it actually does. In fact, U.S. aid has declined steadily since the Cold War ended, to a fraction of 1 percent of the federal budget. Twenty-one other industrial nations devote a greater percentage of their national income to foreign assistance than the United States does.

Foreign Aid to End Hunger urges President George W. Bush and Congress to allocate an additional $1 billion a year in U.S. development aid for Africa, where hunger is deep, pervasive, and widespread.

Bread for the World Institute believes moral obligation is reason enough. But strengthening Africa's economies would open new markets for U.S. businesses and create a far more stable world, reducing the likelihood of costly U.S. military or humanitarian interventions.

The need is great. In sub-Saharan Africa, 291 million people (more than the entire U.S. population) live on less than $1 a day, and one person in three is chronically undernourished. In all, more than 186 million Africans are malnourished.

HIV/AIDS is causing widespread sickness and death. Two-thirds of the 23 million people living with HIV/AIDS worldwide are in sub-Saharan Africa. AIDS has orphaned 12 million African children.

Sub-Saharan Africa also contends with civil wars, low agricultural production, scarce health care, inadequate education, environmental degradation, poor roads, and lack of sanitation. Debt to foreign creditors and international financial institutions also causes immense suffering, siphoning funds that could be spent on desperately needed human services.

Despite these obstacles, Africa is showing signs of renewal. In many countries, democratic governments have replaced dictatorships. New businesses and private investment are growing. Women are gaining a role in economic and political life. African governments are fighting HIV/AIDS aggressively.

To build on these positive trends, Bread for the World Institute advocates a long-term U.S. aid partnership to reduce hunger and strengthen Africa's capacity to solve its own problems. Projects would be planned and run by Africans, with technical assistance from U.S. and international agricultural and business advisors. African governments would provide leadership, stability, and sound economic policies.

Based on Africa's documented needs and on lessons learned from successful development programs, *Foreign Aid to End Hunger* recommends that Africa use U.S. aid to:

Invest in agriculture, the surest way to end hunger in the long term. Sub-Saharan Africa's food production has declined 23 percent in the past 25 years. But U.S. aid could fund agricultural research and extension services to help farmers improve crop yields. With new farming methods, African nations could grow more food for their own people and also earn income by exporting. The research institutes that made Asia's Green Revolution possible are now developing improved crop varieties and cultivation techniques for Africa. African farmers also need better access to land, capital, and livestock.

Build good roads and infrastructure. Poor or nonexistent roads make it difficult to deliver food to hungry people. Farmers need roads to take their crops to market and to obtain fertilizer, tools, seeds, and other supplies. Food processing companies and other industries could open plants in rural areas, near the farmers, if communities had good roads, electric power, clean water, sanitation, and telecommunications.

Enroll more children in school and keep them there. Sub-Saharan nations generally have low literacy rates, low school enrollment, and too few classrooms and teachers. But U.S. funds could help correct this and enable more girls to get an education.

Empower and educate African women. This one step would have a profound effect on the way African families live. Women working small plots of land produce 70 percent of Africa's food. Yet women are often denied the right to own land, obtain farm loans, or start home-based businesses. Girls are frequently kept out of school, even though households run by educated women have more income, better nutrition, higher literacy, and lower birth rates.

Prevent and treat HIV/AIDS, malaria, tuberculosis, and other infectious diseases. U.S. aid could help Africa in its fight against HIV/AIDS by strengthening primary health care, training more doctors, making medicine available, and promoting health education. Doctors are already scarce in Africa, and it is estimated that 25 percent of the region's physicians could die of AIDS in less than five years.

Foster the development of new African-owned businesses and microenterprises. Small, home-based businesses can boost household income, teach people new skills, and enable families to keep children in school. U.S. aid could supply loans and technical training to help launch these enterprises.

Continue debt relief. Reducing the foreign debt payments of the world's poorest nations, most of them in Africa, will free more money for needed social investments and development.

Foreword

The United States could do its part to end world hunger for a penny per day per U.S. citizen. That doesn't sound like much. But it adds up to $1 billion each year to help hungry people.

Hunger is a problem we can actually solve and we have made great progress. There are fewer undernourished people in the developing world today than 25 years ago, except in Africa, where the extent and depth of hunger have been increasing.

What's needed to support what developing countries are doing to reduce hunger? Effective debt relief for the poorest countries, modest changes in the rules of international trade and finance, and an increase in poverty-focused foreign aid. The increase would cost the industrialized countries about $4 billion annually, and the U.S. share would be $1 billion annually.

Bread for the World Institute's sister organization, Bread for the World, lobbies Congress for laws to reduce hunger. When Bread for the World members ask their representatives in Congress for more foreign aid for poor people in developing countries, questions arise about whether the money will be well spent. With good reason: most foreign aid hasn't helped poor people. In fact, most foreign aid wasn't even intended to help poor people. It was designed mainly to win friends during the Cold War, support Israel and Middle East peace, and promote business and foreign policy interests.

Aid that focused on reducing poverty often worked, and experience has yielded lessons about how to make it work better. Now that the Cold War is over, official aid agencies such as the United States Agency for International Development and the World Bank are focusing more on poverty reduction and grassroots participation. Most importantly, democracy and economic pragmatism have become much more prevalent throughout the developing world.

Under these circumstances, it is feasible to mount an international effort to accelerate progress against hunger. The effort would concentrate on Africa. It would include programs to combat AIDS, provide schooling for all children, strengthen farming and small businesses, and promote peace and good government. Poor countries – mainly the families who struggle every day to feed themselves – will do most of what it takes to overcome world hunger. But assistance from the world's richest countries could give them a huge boost.

Various methodologies suggest that $4 billion a year would be enough to achieve the internationally agreed target of cutting hunger in half by 2015. Small amounts of money, by U.S. standards, can go a long way in Africa. For example, $1,000 will cover a teacher's salary for a year. That extra teacher will allow more children to attend school. Most of the children who are now kept home are girls, and educating girls is a powerful way to improve family life, nutrition, and agriculture.

The United States, the most powerful of the industrialized countries, is often the least generous. So when the United States proposes an initiative to help developing countries, other

industrialized countries are typically willing to support it. When the United States agreed to debt reduction for poor countries, for example, the other industrialized countries – and the developing countries, too – rallied around the U.S. plan.

Moreover, U.S. presidents of both parties have usually been more willing to help developing countries than Congress. If the U.S. Congress would approve a commitment of $1 billion a year for the next 15 years, President George W. Bush could lead the global initiative needed to overcome hunger.

Last year, Bread for the World's grassroots members across the country and allied groups convinced Congress to approve debt relief for the poorest countries and increase nutrition assistance for hungry people in this country. These were significant steps in our program to end hunger. They showed that concerned people at the grassroots can overcome partisan gridlock. We can get members of Congress from both parties to come together to help hungry people.

In 2001, Bread for the World will be campaigning to increase effective aid to Africa. The campaign is called *Africa: Hunger to Harvest*. How Congress responds will depend on what citizens back home say they want. So if you want the United States to do its part to end world hunger, find out about Bread for the World's campaign and let your members of Congress know what you think.

David Beckmann
President
Bread for the World and
Bread for the World Institute